LUNCH POEMS

Frank O'Hara

CITY LIGHTS BOOKS
The Pocket Poets Series : Number 19

Library of Congress Catalog Card Number : 64-8689.

The Pocket Poets Series is published at the City Lights Bookstore, 261 Columbus Avenue, San Francisco, California 94133, USA.

CONTENTS

to Joseph LeSueur

Some of these poems have appeared previously in *Yugen, Evergreen Review, Poetry, Locus Solus, The Beat Scene, Big Table, Signal, Nugget, The Floating Bear, C, The New American Poetry,* and *City Lights Journal,* to all of whom the author and publisher offer their thanks.

MUSIC

If I rest for a moment near The Equestrian
pausing for a liver sausage sandwich in the Mayflower Shoppe,
that angel seems to be leading the horse into Bergdorf's
and I am naked as a table cloth, my nerves humming.
Close to the fear of war and the stars which have disappeared.
I have in my hands only 35c, it's so meaningless to eat!
and gusts of water spray over the basins of leaves
like the hammers of a glass pianoforte. If I seem to you
to have lavender lips under the leaves of the world,
     I must tighten my belt.
It's like a locomotive on the march, the season
     of distress and clarity
and my door is open to the evenings of midwinter's
lightly falling snow over the newspapers.
Clasp me in your handkerchief like a tear, trumpet
of early afternoon! in the foggy autumn.
As they're putting up the Christmas trees on Park Avenue
I shall see my daydreams walking by with dogs in blankets,
put to some use before all those coloured lights come on!
     But no more fountains and no more rain,
     and the stores stay open terribly late.

1953

ALMA

"Est-elle almée? . . . aux premières heures bleues
Se détruira-t-elle comme les fleurs feues. . . ."
— Rimbaud.

1
The sun, perhaps three of them, one black one red, you know,
and her dancing all the time, fanning the purple sky getting
purple, her fancy white skin quite unoriental to the dirty child-
ren's round eyes standing in circles munching muffins, the cock-
roaches like nuggets half hid in the bran. Boy! how are you,
Prester John? the smile of the river, so searching, so enamelled.

2
What mention of the King?
the spinning wheel still turns,
the apples rot to the singing,
Alceste on winter sojourns

is nice at Nice. Wander,
my dear sacred Pontiff, do dare
to murder minutely and ponder
what is the bloody affair

inside the heart of the weak
dancer, whose one toe is worth
inestimable, the gang, the cheek
of it! it's too dear, her birth

amidst the acorns with nails
stuck through them by passionate

parents, castanets! Caucasian tales!
their prodigality proportionate :

"Sacred Heart, oh Heart so sick,
make Detroit more wholly thine,
all with greeds and scabs so thick
that Judas Priest must make a sign."

Thus he to bed and we to rise
and Alma singing like a loon.
Her dancing toenails in her eyes.
Her pa was dead on the River Gaboon.

3

Detroit was founded on the great near waterways next to Canada
which was friendly and immediately gained for herself the appel-
lation "the Detroit of Thermopylaes", a name which has stuck to
this day wherever ballroom dancing is held in proper esteem. Let
me remind you of that great wrist movement, the enjambement
schizophrene, a particularly satisfying variation of which may be
made by adding a little tomato paste. Great success. While in
Detroit accused of starting the Chicago fire. Millions of roses
from Russians. Alma had come a long way, she opened a jewelry
shop, her name became a household word, she'd invented an
arch-supporter.

How often she thought of her father! the castle, the kitchen-
garden, the hollihocks and the mill stream beyond curving gently
as a parenthesis. Many a bitter tear was shed by her on the
boards of this theatre as she pondered the inscrutable meagerness
of divine Providence, always humming, always shifting a little,
never missing a beat. She guested one season at the height of her
nostalgia with the Metropolitan Opera Ballet in *Salammbô*; her

father seemed very close in all that oriental splendor of bamboo and hotel palms and stale sweat and bracelets, an engagement of tears. In the snow, in her white fox fur wraps, how more beautiful than Mary Garden!

4
Onward to the West. "Where I came from,
where I'm going. Indian country." Gold.
Oh say can you see Alma. The darling
of Them. All her friends were artists.
They alone have memories. They alone
love flowers. They alone give parties
and die. Poor Alma. They alone.
                                    She died,
and it was as if all the jewels in the world
had heaved a sigh. The seismograph
at Fordham University registered, for once,
a spiritual note. How like a sliver
in her own short fat muscular foot.
She loved the Western World, though
there are some who say she isn't really dead.

                                                    1953

ON RACHMANINOFF'S BIRTHDAY

Quick ! a last poem before I go
off my rocker. Oh Rachmaninoff !
Onset, Massachusetts. Is it the fig-newton
playing the horn? Thundering windows
of hell, will your tubes ever break
into powder? Oh my palace of oranges,
junk shop, staples, umber, basalt;
I'm a child again when I was really
miserable, a grope pizzicato. My pocket
of rhinestone, yoyo, carpenter's pencil,
amethyst, hypo, campaign button,
is the room full of smoke? Shit
on the soup, let it burn. So it's back.
You'll never be mentally sober.

1953

POEM

I watched an armory combing its bronze bricks
and in the sky there were glistening rails of milk.
Where had the swan gone, the one with the lame back?

> Now mounting the steps
> I enter my new home full
> of grey radiators and glass
> ashtrays full of wool.

Against the winter I must get a samovar
embroidered with basil leaves and Ukranian mottos
to the distant sound of wings, painfully anti-wind,

> a little bit of the blue
> summer air will come back
> as the steam chuckles in
> the monster's steamy attack

and I'll be happy here and happy there, full
of tea and tears. I don't suppose I'll ever get
to Italy, but I have the terrible tundra at least.

> My new home will be full
> of wood, roots and the like,
> while I pace in a turtleneck
> sweater, repairing my bike.

I watched the palisades shivering in the snow
of my face, which had grown preternaturally pure.
Once I destroyed a man's idea of himself to have him.

If I'd had a samovar then
I'd have made him tea
and as hyacinths grow from
a pot he would love me

and my charming room of tea cosies full of dirt
which is why I must travel, to collect the leaves.
O my enormous piano, you are not like being outdoors

though it is cold and you
are made of fire and wood !
I lift your lid and mountains
return, that I am good.

The stars blink like a hairnet that was dropped
on a seat and now it is lying in the alley behind
the theater where my play is echoed by dying voices.

I am really a woodcarver
and my words are love
which willfully parades in
its room, refusing to move.

1954

ON THE WAY TO SAN REMO

The black ghinkos snarl their way up
the moon growls at each blinking window
the apartment houses climb deafeningly into the purple

> A bat hisses northwards
> the perilous steps lead to a grate
> suddenly the heat is bearable

The cross-eyed dog scratches a worn patch of pavement
his right front leg is maimed in the shape of a V
there's no trace of his nails on the street a woman cajoles

> She is very old and dirty
> she whistles her filthy hope
> that it will rain tonight

The 6th Avenue bus trunk-lumbers sideways
it is full of fat people who cough as at a movie
they eat each other's dandruff in the flickering glare

> The moon passes into clouds
> so hurt by the street lights
> of your glance oh my heart

The act of love is also passing like a subway bison
through the paper-littered arches of the express tracks
the sailor sobers he feeds pennies to the peanut machines

> Though others are in the night
> far away lips upon a dusty armpit
> the nostrils are full of tears

High fidelity reposed in a box a hand on the windowpane
the sweet calm the violin strings tie a young man's hair
the bright black eyes pin far away their smudged curiosity

> Yes you are foolish smoking
> the bars are for rabbits
> who wish to outlive the men

1954

2 POEMS FROM THE OHARA MONOGATARI

1
My love is coming in a glass
the blood of the Bourbons

saxophone or cornet
qu'importe où?

green of glass flowers dans le Kentucky

and always the same handkerchief
at the same nose of damask

turning up my extravagant collar
tossing my scarf about my neck

the Baudelaire of Kyoto's never-ending pureness
is he cracked in the head?

2
After a long trip to a shrine
in wooden clogs so hard on the muscles
the tea is bitter and the breasts are hard
so much terrace for one evening

there is no longer no ocean
I don't see the ocean under my stilts
as I poke along

hands on ankles feet on wrists
naked in thought
like a whip made from sheerest stockings

the radio is on the cigarette is puffed upon
by the pleasures of rolling in a bog
some call the Milky Way
in far-fetched Occidental lands above the trees
where dwell the amusing skulls

1954

A STEP AWAY FROM THEM

It's my lunch hour, so I go
for a walk among the hum-colored
cabs. First, down the sidewalk
where laborers feed their dirty
glistening torsos sandwiches
and Coca-Cola, with yellow helmets
on. They protect them from falling
bricks, I guess. Then onto the
avenue where skirts are flipping
above heels and blow up over
grates. The sun is hot, but the
cabs stir up the air. I look
at bargains in wristwatches. There
are cats playing in sawdust.
                                                On

to Times Square, where the sign
blows smoke over my head, and higher
the waterfall pours lightly. A
Negro stands in a doorway with a
toothpick, languorously agitating.
A blonde chorus girl clicks : he
smiles and rubs his chin. Everything
suddenly honks : it is 12 :40 of
a Thursday.
                  Neon in daylight is a
great pleasure, as Edwin Denby would
write, as are light bulbs in daylight.
I stop for a cheeseburger at JULIET'S
CORNER. Giulietta Masina, wife of
Federico Fellini, *è bell' attrice.*

And chocolate malted. A lady in
foxes on such a day puts her poodle
in a cab.
   There are several Puerto
Ricans on the avenue today, which
makes it beautiful and warm. First
Bunny died, then John Latouche,
then Jackson Pollock. But is the
earth as full as life was full, of them?
And one has eaten and one walks,
past the magazines with nudes
and the posters for BULLFIGHT and
the Manhattan Storage Warehouse,
which they'll soon tear down. I
used to think they had the Armory
Show there.
   A glass of papaya juice
and back to work. My heart is in my
pocket, it is Poems by Pierre Reverdy.

1956

CAMBRIDGE

It is still raining and the yellow-green cotton fruit
looks silly round a window giving out on winter trees
with only three drab leaves left. The hot plate works,
it is the sole heat on earth, and instant coffee. I
put on my warm corduroy pants, a heavy maroon sweater,
and wrap myself in my old maroon bathrobe. Just like Pasternak
in Marburg (they say Italy and France are colder, but
I'm sure that Germany's at least as cold as this) and,
lacking the Master's inspiration, I may freeze to death
before I can get out into the white rain. I could have left
the window closed last night? But that's where health
comes from! His breath from the Urals, drawing me into flame
like a forgotten cigarette. Burn! this is not negligible,
being poetic, and not feeble, since it's sponsored by
the greatest living Russian poet at incalculable cost.
Across the street there is a house under construction,
abandoned to the rain. Secretly, I shall go to work on it

1956

POEM

Instant coffee with slightly sour cream
in it, and a phone call to the beyond
which doesn't seem to be coming any nearer.
" Ah daddy, I wanna stay drunk many days "
on the poetry of a new friend
my life held precariously in the seeing
hands of others, their and my impossibilities.
Is this love, now that the first love
has finally died, where there were no impossibilities?

1956

THREE AIRS

to Norman Bluhm

1.
So many things in the air! soot,
elephant balls, a Chinese cloud
which is entirely collapsed, a cat
swung by its tail
                    and the senses
of the dead which are banging about
inside my tired red eyes

2.
In the deeps there is a little bird
and it only hums, it hums of fortitude

and temperance, it is managing a foundry

how firmly it must grasp things! tear them
out of the slime and then, alas! it mischievously

drops them into the cauldron of hideousness

there is already a sunset naming
the poplars which see only, watery, themselves

3.
Oh to be an angel (if there were any!), and go
straight up into the sky and look around and then come down

not to be covered with steel and aluminum
glaringly ugly in the pure distances and clattering and
                              buckling, wheezing

but to be part of the treetops and the blueness, invisible,
the iridescent darknesses beyond,
                         silent, listening to
               the air becoming no air becoming air again
                                               1958

IMAGE OF THE BUDDHA PREACHING

I am very happy to be here at the Villa Hügel
and Prime Minister Nehru has asked me to greet the people of
Essen

and to tell you how powerfully affected we in India
have been by Germany's philosophy, traditions and mythology
though our lucidity and our concentration on archetypes
puts us in a class by ourself
"for in this world of storm and stress "
— 5,000 years of Indian art ! just think of it, oh Essen !
is this a calmer region of thought, " a reflection of the mind
through the ages " ?
Max Müller, " primus inter pares " among
Indologists
remember our byword, Mokshamula, I rejoice in the fact of 900
exhibits

I deeply appreciate filling the gaps, oh Herr Doktor Heinrich
Goetz !
and the research purring onward in Pakistan and Ceylon and
Afghanistan
soapstone, terracotta-Indus, terracotta-Maurya, terracotta Sunga,
terracotta-Andhra, terracotta fragments famous Bharhut
Stupa
Kushana, Ghandara, Gupta, Hindu and Jain, Secco, Ajanta,
Villa Hügel !

Anglo-German trade will prosper by Swansea-Mannheim
friendship
waning now the West Wall by virtue of two rolls per capita
and the flagship BERLIN is joining its "white fleet" on the Rhine

though better schools and model cars are wanting, still still oh

Essen

    Nataraja dances on the dwarf
    and unlike their fathers
    Germany's highschool pupils love the mathematics

    which is hopeful of a new delay in terror
    I don't think

1959

SONG

Is it dirty
does it look dirty
that's what you think of in the city

does it just seem dirty
that's what you think of in the city
you don't refuse to breathe do you

someone comes along with a very bad character
he seems attractive. is he really. yes. very
he's attractive as his character is bad. is it. yes

that's what you think of in the city
run your finger along your no-moss mind
that's not a thought that's soot

and you take a lot of dirt off someone
is the character less bad. no. it improves constantly
you don't refuse to breathe do you

                                                          1959

THE DAY LADY DIED

It is 12 : 20 in New York a Friday
three days after Bastille day, yes
it is 1959 and I go get a shoeshine
because I will get off the 4 : 19 in Easthampton
at 7 : 15 and then go straight to dinner
and I don't know the people who will feed me

I walk up the muggy street beginning to sun
and have a hamburger and a malted and buy
an ugly NEW WORLD WRITING to see what the poets
in Ghana are doing these days
                        I go on to the bank
and Miss Stillwagon (first name Linda I once heard)
doesn't even look up my balance for once in her life
and in the GOLDEN GRIFFIN I get a little Verlaine
for Patsy with drawings by Bonnard although I do
think of Hesiod, trans. Richmond Lattimore or
Brendan Behan's new play or *Le Balcon* or *Les Nègres*
of Genet, but I don't, I stick with Verlaine
after practically going to sleep with quandariness

and for Mike I just stroll into the PARK LANE
Liquor Store and ask for a bottle of Strega and
then I go back where I came from to 6th Avenue
and the tobacconist in the Ziegfeld Theatre and
casually ask for a carton of Gauloises and a carton
of Picayunes, and a NEW YORK POST with her face on it

and I am sweating a lot by now and thinking of
leaning on the john door in the 5 SPOT
while she whispered a song along the keyboard
to Mal Waldron and everyone and I stopped breathing

                                                    1959

POEM

Wouldn't it be funny
if The Finger had designed us
to shit just once a week?

      all week long we'd get fatter
      and fatter and then on Sunday morning
      while everyone's in church

                ploop!

                  1959

POEM

Khrushchev is coming on the right day!

        the cool graced light
is pushed off the enormous glass piers by hard wind
and everything is tossing, hurrying on up

       this country
has everything but *politesse,* a Puerto Rican cab driver says
and five different girls I see

      look like Piedie Gimbel
with her blonde hair tossing too,

       as she looked when I pushed
her little daughter on the swing on the lawn it was also windy

last night we went to a movie and came out,

       Ionesco is greater
than Beckett, Vincent said, that's what I think, blueberry blintzes
and Khrushchev was probably being carped at

      in Washington, no
        politesse
Vincent tells me about his mother's trip to Sweden

       Hans tells us
about his father's life in Sweden, it sounds like Grace Hartigan's
painting *Sweden*

     so I go home to bed and names drift through my
        head
Purgatorio Merchado, Gerhard Schwartz and Gaspar Gonzales,
  all unknown figures of the early morning as I go to work

where does the evil of the year go

      when September takes New York
and turns it into ozone stalagmites

          deposits of light
          so I get back up
make coffee, and read François Villon, his life, so dark
   New York seems blinding and my tie is blowing up the street
I wish it would blow off
        though it is cold and somewhat warms
                 my neck
as the train bears Khrushchev on to Pennsylvania Station
   and the light seems to be eternal
   and joy seems to be inexorable
   I am foolish enough always to find it in wind

                       1959

NAPHTHA

Ah Jean Dubuffet
when you think of him
doing his military service in the Eiffel Tower
as a meteorologist
in 1922
you know how wonderful the 20th Century
can be
and the gaited Iroquois on the girders
fierce and unflinching-footed
nude as they should be
slightly empty
like a Sonia Delaunay
there is a parable of speed
somewhere behind the Indians' eyes
they invented the century with their horses
and their fragile backs
which are dark

we owe a debt to the Iroquois
and to Duke Ellington
for playing in the buildings when they are built
we don't do much ourselves
but fuck and think
of the haunting Métro
and the one who didn't show up there
while we were waiting to become part of our century
just as you can't make a hat out of steel
and still wear it
who wears hats anyway
it is our tribe's custom
to beguile

how are you feeling in ancient September
I am feeling like a truck on a wet highway
how can you
you were made in the image of god
I was not
I was made in the image of a sissy truck-driver
and Jean Dubuffet painting his cows
"with a likeness burst in the memory"
apart from love (don't say it)
I am ashamed of my century
for being so entertaining
but I have to smile

1959

PERSONAL POEM

Now when I walk around at lunchtime
I have only two charms in my pocket
an old Roman coin Mike Kanemitsu gave me
and a bolt-head that broke off a packing case
when I was in Madrid the others never
brought me too much luck though they did
help keep me in New York against coercion
but now I'm happy for a time and interested

I walk through the luminous humidity
passing the House of Seagram with its wet
and its loungers and the construction to
the left that closed the sidewalk if
I ever get to be a construction worker
I'd like to have a silver hat please
and get to Moriarty's where I wait for
LeRoi and hear who wants to be a mover and
shaker the last five years my batting average
is .016 that's that, and LeRoi comes in
and tells me Miles Davis was clubbed 12
times last night outside BIRDLAND by a cop
a lady asks us for a nickel for a terrible
disease but we don't give her one we
don't like terrible diseases, then

we go eat some fish and some ale it's
cool but crowded we don't like Lionel Trilling
we decide, we like Don Allen we don't like
Henry James so much we like Herman Melville
we don't want to be in the poets' walk in
San Francisco even we just want to be rich
and walk on girders in our silver hats
I wonder if one person out of the 8,000,000 is
thinking of me as I shake hands with LeRoi
and buy a strap for my wristwatch and go
back to work happy at the thought possibly so

1959

ADIEU TO NORMAN,
BON JOUR TO JOAN AND JEAN-PAUL

It is 12 : 10 in New York and I am wondering
if I will finish this in time to meet Norman for lunch
ah lunch ! I think I am going crazy
what with my terrible hangover and the weekend coming up
at excitement-prone Kenneth Koch's
I wish I were staying in town and working on my poems
at Joan's studio for a new book by Grove Press
which they will probably not print
but it is good to be several floors up in the dead of night
wondering whether you are any good or not
and the only decision you can make is that you did it

yesterday I looked up the rue Frémicourt on a map
and was happy to find it like a bird
flying over Paris et ses environs
which unfortunately did not include Seine-et-Oise

                                       which I don't know

as well as a number of other things
and Allen is back talking about god a lot
and Peter is back not talking very much
and Joe has a cold and is not coming to Kenneth's
although he is coming to lunch with Norman
I suspect he is making a distinction
well, who isn't

I wish I were reeling around Paris
instead of reeling around New York
I wish I weren't reeling at all
it is Spring the ice has melted the Ricard is being poured

we are all happy and young and toothless
it is the same as old age
the only thing to do is simply continue
is that simple
yes, it is simple because it is the only thing to do
can you do it
yes, you can because it is the only thing to do
blue light over the Bois de Boulogne it continues
the Seine continues
the Louvre stays open it continues it hardly closes at all
the Bar Américain continues to be French
de Gaulle continues to be Algerian as does Camus
Shirley Goldfarb continues to be Shirley Goldfarb
and Jane Hazan continues to be Jane Freilicher (I think !)
and Irving Sandler continues to be the balayeur des artistes
and so do I (sometimes I think I'm "in love" with painting)
and surely the Piscine Deligny continues to have water in it
and the Flore continues to have tables and newspapers
                              and people under them
and surely we shall not continue to be unhappy
we shall be happy
but we shall continue to be ourselves everything
                              continues to be possible
René Char, Pierre Reverdy, Samuel Beckett it is possible isn't it
I love Reverdy for saying yes, though I don't believe it

                                          1959

RHAPSODY

515 Madison Avenue
door to heaven? portal
stopped realities and eternal licentiousness
or at least the jungle of impossible eagerness
your marble is bronze and your lianas elevator cables
swinging from the myth of ascending
I would join
or declining the challenge of racial attractions
they zing on (into the lynch, dear friends)
while everywhere love is breathing draftily
like a doorway linking 53rd with 54th
the east-bound with the west-bound traffic by 8,000,000s
o midtown tunnels and the tunnels, too, of Holland

where is the summit where all aims are clear
the pin-point light upon a fear-of lust
as agony's needlework grows up around the unicorn
and fences him for milk- and yoghurt-work
when I see Gianni I know he's thinking of John Ericson
playing the Rachmaninoff 2nd or Elizabeth Taylor
taking sleeping-pills and Jane thinks of Manderley
and Irkutsk while I cough lightly in the smog of desire
and my eyes water achingly imitating the true blue

a sight of Manahatta in the towering needle
multi-faceted insight of the fly in the stringless labyrinth
Canada plans a higher place than the Empire State Building
I am getting into a cab at 9th Street and 1st Avenue
and the Negro driver tells me about a $120 apartment
"where you can't walk across the floor after 10 at night
not even to pee, cause it keeps them awake downstairs"
no, I don't like that "well, I didn't take it"
perfect in the hot humid morning on my way to work
a little supper-club conversation for the mill of the gods

you were there always and you know all about these things
as indifferent as an encyclopedia with your calm brown eyes
it isn't enough to smile when you run the gauntlet
you've got to spit like Niagara Falls on everybody or
Victoria Falls or at least the beautiful urban fountains of Madrid
as the Niger joins the Gulf of Guinea near the Menemsha Bar
that is what you learn in the early morning passing
                                        Madison Avenue
where you've never spent any time and stores eat up light

I have always wanted to be near it
though the day is long (and I don't mean Madison Avenue)
lying in a hammock on St. Mark's Place sorting my poems
in the rancid nourishment of this mountainous island
they are coming and we holy ones must go
is Tibet historically a part of China? as I historically
belong to the enormous bliss of American death

                                                    1959

HOTEL PARTICULIER

How exciting it is
                    not to be at Port Lligat
or learning Portuguese in Bilbao so you can go to Brazil

Erik Satie made a great mistake learning Latin
the Brise Marine wasn't written in Sanskrit, baby

I had a teacher one whole summer who never told me anything
                                      and it was wonderful

and then there is the Bibliothèque Nationale, cuspidors,
glasses, anxiety
                    you don't get crabs that way,
and what you don't know will hurt somebody else

how clear the air is, how low the moon, how flat the sun,
et cetera,
                    just so you don't coin a phrase that changes
can be "rung" on
                    like les neiges d'antan
and that sort of thing (oops !), (roll me over) !

is this the hostel where the lazy and fun-loving
                            start up the mountain?

                                                      1960

CORNKIND

So the rain falls
it drops all over the place
and where it finds a little rock pool
it fills it up with dirt
and the corn grows
a green Bette Davis sits under it
reading a volume of William Morris
oh fertility! beloved of the Western world
you aren't so popular in China
though they fuck too

and do I really want a son
to carry on my idiocy past the Horned Gates
poor kid   a staggering load

yet it can happen casually
and he lifts a little of the load each day
as I become more and more idiotic
and grows to be a strong strong man
and one day carries as I die
my final idiocy and the very gates
into a future of his choice

but what of William Morris
what of you Million Worries
what of Bette Davis in
AN EVENING WITH WILLIAM MORRIS
or THE WORLD OF SAMUEL GREENBERG

what of Hart Crane
what of phonograph records and gin

what of "what of"

you are of me, that's what
and that's the meaning of fertility
hard and moist and moaning

1960

HOW TO GET THERE

White the October air, no snow, easy to breathe
beneath the sky, lies, lies everywhere writhing and gasping
clutching and tangling, it is not easy to breathe
lies building their tendrils into dim figures
who disappear down corridors in west-side apartments
into childhood's proof of being wanted, not abandoned, kidnapped
betrayal staving off loneliness, I see the fog lunge in
and hide it
           where are you?
                      here I am on the sidewalk
under the moonlike lamplight thinking how precious moss is
so unique and greenly crushable if you can find it
on the north side of the tree where the fog binds you
and then, tearing apart into soft white lies, spreads its disease
through the primal night of an everlasting winter
which nevertheless has heat in tubes, west-side and east-side
and its intricate individual pathways of white accompanied
by the ringing of telephone bells beside which someone sits in
silence denying their own number, never given out! nameless
like the sound of troika bells rushing past suffering
in the first storm, it is snowing now, it is already too late
the snow will go away, but nobody will be there

police cordons for lying political dignitaries ringing too
the world becomes a jangle
                        from the index finger
to the vast empty houses filled with people, their echoes

of lies and the tendrils of fog trailing softly around their throats
now the phone can be answered, nobody calling, only an echo
all can confess to be home and waiting, all is the same
and we drift into the clear sky enthralled by our disappointment
       never to be alone again
                    never to be loved
sailing through space : didn't I have you once for my self?
                          West Side?
   for a couple of hours, but I am not that person
                        1960

A LITTLE TRAVEL DIARY

Wending our way through the gambas, angulas,
the merluzas that taste like the Sea Post on Sunday
and the great quantities of huevos they take off
Spanish Naval officers' uniforms and put on plates,
and reach the gare de Francia in the gloaming
with my ton of books and John's ton of clothes bought
in a wild fit of enthusiasm in Madrid; all jumbled
together like life is a Jumble Shop

                              of the theatre
in Spain they said nothing for foreigners
and we head in our lovely 1st class coach, shifting
and sagging, towards the northwest, while in other compartments
Dietrich and Erich von Stroheim share a sandwich of chorizos
and a bottle of Vichy Catalan, in the dining car
the travelling gentleman with linear mustache and many
many rings rolls his cigar around and drinks Martini y
ginebra, and Lillian Gish rolls on over the gorges
with a tear in her left front eye, comme Picasso,
through the night through the night, longitudinous
and affected with stars; the riverbeds so far below look
as a pig's tongue on a platter, and storms break over
San Sebastian, 40 foot waves drench us pleasantly and we see
a dead dog bloated as a fraise lolling beside the quai
and slowly pulling out to sea

                         to Irun and Biarritz
we go, sapped of anxiety, and there for the first time
since arriving in Barcelona I can freely shit
and the surf is so high and the sun is so hot
and it was all built yesterday as everything should be

what a splendid country it is

                          full of indecision and cognac
and bikinis, sens plastiques (ugh ! hooray !); see the back
of the head of Bill Berkson, aux Deux Magots, (awk !) it gleams
like the moon through the smoke of the Renfe as we passed
through the endless tunnels and the silver vistas
of our quest for the rocher de la Vierge and salt spray

                                                1960

FIVE POEMS

Well now, hold on
maybe I won't go to sleep at all
and it'll be a beautiful white night
or else I'll collapse
completely from nerves and be calm
as a rug or a bottle of pills
or suddenly I'll be off Montauk
swimming and loving it and not caring where

*   *   *

an invitation to lunch
HOW DO YOU LIKE THAT?
when I only have 16 cents and 2
packages of yoghurt
there's a lesson in that, isn't there
like in Chinese poetry when a leaf falls?
hold off on the yoghurt till the very
last, when everything may improve

*   *   *

at the Rond-Point they were eating
a oyster, but here
we were dropping by sculptures
and seeing some paintings
and the smasheroo-grates of Cadoret
and music by Varèse, too
well Adolph Gottlieb I guess you

are the hero of this day
along with venison and Bill

I'll sleep on the yoghurt and dream of the Persian Gulf

        *   *   *

which I did it was wonderful
to be in bed again and the knock
on my door for once signified "hi there"
and on the deafening walk
through the ghettos where bombs have gone off lately
left by subway violators
I knew why I love taxis, yes
subways are only fun when you're feeling sexy
and who feels sexy after *The Blue Angel*
well maybe a little bit

        *   *   *

I seem to be defying fate, or am I avoiding it?

1960

AVE MARIA

Mothers of America
          let your kids go to the movies!
get them out of the house so they won't know what you're up to
it's true that fresh air is good for the body
          but what about the soul
that grows in darkness, embossed by silvery images
and when you grow old as grow old you must
          they won't hate you
they won't criticise you they won't know
          they'll be in some glamorous country
they first saw on a Saturday afternoon or playing hookey

they may even be grateful to you
          for their first sexual experience
which only cost you a quarter
          and didn't upset the peaceful home
they will know where candy bars come from
          and gratuitous bags of popcorn
as gratuitous as leaving the movie before it's over
with a pleasant stranger whose apartment is in the
          Heaven on Earth Bldg
near the Williamsburg Bridge
          oh mothers you will have made the little tykes
so happy because if nobody does pick them up in the movies
they won't know the difference
          and if somebody does it'll be sheer gravy
and they'll have been truly entertained either way
instead of hanging around the yard
          or up in their room
          hating you

prematurely since you won't have done anything horribly

                                                            mean yet

except keeping them from the darker joys

                                            it's unforgivable the latter

so don't blame me if you won't take this advice

                                            and the family breaks up

and your children grow old and blind in front of a TV set

                                                  seeing

movies you wouldn't let them see when they were young

                                                      1960

PISTACHIO TREE AT CHATEAU NOIR

Beaucoup de musique classique et moderne Guillaume and not
as one may imagine it sounds not in the ear
what went was attributed to wandering aimlessly off
what came arrived simply for itself and inflamed me
yet I do not explain what exactly makes me so happy today
any more than I can explain the unseasonal warmth
of my unhabitual heart pumping vulgarly the blood
of another I loved another and now my love is other
my love is in the movies downstairs and yesterday
bought ice cream and looked for a pigeon-menaced owl
mais, Guillaume, où es-tu, Guillaume, comme les musiques

and like the set for *Rigoletto* like the set for *Roma*
like so many sets one's heart is torn like Berman's
spacious haunt where tenors walk in pumps and girls
in great big hats or none at all "or perhaps he recorded
the panorama of hills and valleys before the strangely
naked" and rain is turning the set into a dumpling

wherever I see a "while" I seem to lose a little time
and gradually my feet dragging I slow down the damn bus
it is because of you so I can watch you smile longer
that's what the Spring is and the elbow of noon walks
where did you go who did you see the children proclaim
and they too gradually fill the sepulchre with dolls
and the sepulchre jumps and jounces and turns pink with wrath

1961

AT KAMIN'S DANCE BOOKSHOP

to Vincent Warren

Shade of Fanny Elssler! I dreamt that you passed over me last
                                        night in sleep
was it you who was asleep or was it me? sweet shade
shade shade shill spade agony freak
geek you were not nor were you made of ribbons but of warm
                                        moving flesh & tulle
you were twining your left leg around your right as if your
                                        right were me
I've never felt so wide awake
I seemed to be wearing tights entwined with your legs and a
                                        big sash over my crotch
and a jewel in my left ear for luck
(to help me balance) and you were pulling me toward the floor
                                        reaching for stars
it seemed to me that I was warm at last
and palpable not just a skein of lust dipped in the grand
                                        appreciation of yours
where are you Fanny Elssler come back!

                                        1961

STEPS

How funny you are today New York
like Ginger Rogers in *Swingtime*
and St. Bridget's steeple leaning a little to the left

here I have just jumped out of a bed full of V-days
(I got tired of D-days) and blue you there still
accepts me foolish and free
all I want is a room up there
and you in it
and even the traffic halt so thick is a way
for people to rub up against each other
and when their surgical appliances lock
they stay together
for the rest of the day (what a day)
I go by to check a slide and I say
that painting's not so blue

where's Lana Turner
she's out eating
and Garbo's backstage at the Met
everyone's taking their coat off
so they can show a rib-cage to the rib-watchers
and the park's full of dancers and their tights and shoes
in little bags
who are often mistaken for worker-outers at the West Side Y
why not
the Pittsburgh Pirates shout because they won
and in a sense we're all winning
we're alive

the apartment was vacated by a gay couple
who moved to the country for fun
they moved a day too soon
even the stabbings are helping the population explosion
though in the wrong country
and all those liars have left the U N
the Seagram Building's no longer rivalled in interest
not that we need liquor (we just like it)

and the little box is out on the sidewalk
next to the delicatessen
so the old man can sit on it and drink beer
and get knocked off it by his wife later in the day
while the sun is still shining

oh god it's wonderful
to get out of bed
and drink too much coffee
and smoke too many cigarettes
and love you so much

1961

MARY DESTI'S ASS

In Bayreuth once
we were very good friends of the Wagners
and I stepped in once
for Isadora so perfectly
she would never allow me to dance again
that's the way it was in Bayreuth

the way it was in Hackensack
was different
there one never did anything
and everyone hated you anyway
it was fun, it was clear
you knew where you stood

in Boston you were never really standing
I was usually lying
it was amusing to be lying all
the time for everybody
it was like exercise

it means something to exercise
in Norfolk Virginia
it means you've been to bed with a Nigra
well it is exercise
the only difference is it's better than Boston

I was walking along the street
of Cincinnati
and I met Kenneth Koch's mother
fresh from the Istanbul Hilton
she liked me and I liked her
we both liked Istanbul

then in Waukegan I met a furniture manufacturer
and it wiped out all dreams of pleasantness from my mind
it was like being pushed down hard
on a chair
it was like something horrible you hadn't expected
which is the most horrible thing

and in Singapore I got a dreadful
disease it was amusing to have bumps
except they went into my veins
and rose to the surface like Vesuvius
getting cured was like learning to smoke

yet I always loved Baltimore
the porches which hurt your ass
no, they were the steps
well you have a wet ass anyway
if they'd only stop scrubbing

and Frisco where I saw
Toumanova "the baby ballerina" except
she looked like a cow
I didn't know the history of the ballet yet
not that that taught me much

now if you feel like you want to deal with
Tokyo
you've really got something to handle
it's like Times Square at midnight
you don't know where you're going
but you know

and then in Harbin I knew
how to behave it was glorious that
was love sneaking up on me through the snow
and I felt it was because of all
the postcards and the smiles and kisses and the grunts
that was love but I kept on traveling

1961

ST. PAUL AND ALL THAT

Totally abashed and smiling

                              I walk in
                              sit down and
                              face the frigidaire

            it's April
            no May
            it's May

such little things have to be established in morning
after the big things of night
                        do you want me to come? when
I think of all the things I've been thinking of I feel insane
simply "life in Birmingham is hell"
                              simply "you will miss me
                                    but that's good"
when the tears of a whole generation are assembled
they will only fill a coffee cup
                        just because they evaporate
doesn't mean life has heat
                        "this various dream of living"
I am alive with you
                  full of anxious pleasures and pleasurable anxiety
hardness and softness
                  listening while you talk and talking while you read
I read what you read
                  you do not read what I read
which is right, I am the one with the curiosity
            you read for some mysterious reason
                        I read simply because I am a writer
the sun doesn't necessarily set, sometimes it just disappears

when you're not here someone walks in and says

"hey,

there's no dancer in that bed"

O the Polish summers! those drafts!
those black and white teeth!

you never come when you say you'll come but on the other hand
you do come
1961

MEMOIR OF SERGEI O. . . .

My feet have never been comfortable
since I pulled them out of the Black Sea
and came to your foul country
what fatal day did I dry them off for
travel loathesome travel to a world
even older than the one I grew up in
what fatal day meanwhile back in France
they were stumbling towards the Bastille
and the Princesse de Lamballe was
shuddering as shudderingly as I
with a lot less to lose I still hated
to move sedentary as a roach of Tiflis
never again to go swimming in the nude
publicly little did I know how
awfulness could reach perfection abroad
I even thought I would see a Red Indian
all I saw was lipstick everything cov-
ered with grass or shrouds pretty
shrouds shot with silver and plasma
even the chairs are upholstered to a
smothering perfection of inanity
and there are no chandeliers and there
are no gates to the parks so you don't
know whether you're going in them or
coming out of them that's not relaxing
and so you can't really walk all you can
do is sit and drink coffee and brood
over the lost leaves and refreshing scum
of Georgia Georgia of my heritage
and dismay meanwhile back in my old

country they are renaming everything so
I can't even tell any more which ballet
company I am remembering with so much
pain and the same thing has started
here American Avenue Park Avenue South
Avenue of Chester Conklin Binnie Barnes
Boulevard Avenue of Toby Wing Barbara
Nichols Street where am I what is it
I can't even find a pond small enough
to drown in without being ostentatious
you are ruining your awful country and me
it is not new to do this it is terribly
democratic and ordinary and tired

1961

YESTERDAY DOWN AT THE CANAL

You say that everything is very simple and interesting
it makes me feel very wistful, like reading a great Russian novel
does

I am terribly bored
sometimes it is like seeing a bad movie
other days, more often, it's like having an acute disease of the
kidney

god knows it has nothing to do with the heart
nothing to do with people more interesting than myself
yak yak
that's an amusing thought
how can anyone be more amusing than oneself
how can anyone fail to be
can I borrow your forty-five
I only need one bullet preferably silver
if you can't be interesting at least you can be a legend
(but I hate all that crap)

1961

POEM EN FORME DE SAW

I ducked out of sight behind the saw-mill
nobody saw me because of the falls the gates the sluice the
tourist boats

the children were trailing their fingers in the water
and the swans, regal and smarty, were nipping their "little"
fingers

I heard one swan remark "That was a good nip
though they are not as interesting as sausages" and another
reply "Nor as tasty as those peasants we got away from the
elephant that time"

but I didn't really care for conversation that day
I wanted to be alone
which is why I went to the mill in the first place
now I am alone and hate it
I don't want to just make boards for the rest of my life
I'm distressed
the water is very beautiful but you can't go into it
because of the gunk
and the dog is always rolling over, I like dogs on their "little" feet
I think I may scamper off to Winnipeg to see Raymond
but what'll happen to the mill
I see the cobwebs collecting already
and later those other webs, those awful predatory webs
if I stay right here I will eventually get into the newspapers
like Robert Frost
willow trees, willow trees they remind me of Desdemona
I'm so damned literary
and at the same time the waters rushing past remind me of
nothing

I'm so damned empty
what is all this vessel shit anyway
we are all rushing down the River Happy Times

ducking poling bumping sinking and swimming
and we arrive at the beach
the chaff is sand
alone as a tree bumping another tree in a storm
that's not really being alone, is it, signed The Saw

1961

FOR THE CHINESE NEW YEAR
& FOR BILL BERKSON

One or another
Is lost, since we fall apart
Endlessly, in one motion depart
From each other.
— D. H. Lawrence

Behind New York there's a face
and it's not Sibelius's with a cigar
it was red it was strange and hateful
and then I became a child again
like a nadir or a zenith or a nudnik

what do you think this is my youth
and the aged future that is sweeping me away
carless and gasless under the Sutton
and Beekman Places towards a hellish rage
it is there that face I fear under ramps

it is perhaps the period that ends
the problem as a proposition of days of days
just an attack on the feelings that stay
poised in the hurricane's center that
eye through which only camels can pass

but I do not mean that tenderness doesn't
linger like a Paris afternoon or a wart
something dumb and despicable that I love
because it is silent oh what difference
does it make me into some kind of space statistic

a lot is buried under that smile
a lot of sophistication gone down the drain
to become the mesh of a mythical fish
at which we never stare back never stare back
where there is so much downright forgery

under that I find it restful like a bush
some people are outraged by cleanliness
I hate the lack of smells myself and yet I stay
it is better than being actually present
and the stare can swim away into the past

can adorn it with easy convictions rat
cow tiger rabbit dragon snake horse sheep
monkey rooster dog and pig "Flower Drum Song"
so that nothing is vain not the gelded sand
not the old spangled lotus not my fly

which I have thought about but never really
looked at well that's a certain orderliness
of personality "if you're brought up Protestant
enough a Catholic" oh shit on the beaches so
what if I did look up your trunks and see it

II

then the parallel becomes an eagle parade
of Busby Berkeleyites marching marching half-toe
I suppose it's the happiest moment in infinity
because we're dissipated and tired and fond no
I don't think psychoanalysis shrinks the spleen

here we are and what the hell are we going to do
with it we are going to blow it up like daddy did
only us I really think we should go up for a change
I'm tired of always going down what price glory
it's one of those timeless priceless words like come

well now how does your conscience feel about that
would you rather explore tomorrow with a sponge
there's no need to look for a target you're it
like in childhood when the going was aimed at a
sandwich it all depends on which three of us are there

but here come the prophets with their loosening nails
it is only as blue as the lighting under the piles
I have something portentous to say to you but which
of the papier-mâché languages do you understand you
don't dare to take it off paper much less put it on

yes it is strange that everyone fucks and every-
one mentions it and it's boring too that faded floor
how many teeth have chewed a little piece of the lover's
flesh how many teeth are there in the world it's like
Harpo Marx smiling at a million pianos call that Africa

call it New Guinea call it Poughkeepsie I guess
it's love I guess the season of renunciation is at "hand"
the final fatal hour of turpitude and logic demise
is when you miss getting rid of something delouse
is when you don't louse something up which way is the inn

III

I'm looking for a million-dollar heart in a carton
of frozen strawberries like the Swedes where is sunny England
and those fields where they still-birth the wars why
did they suddenly stop playing why is Venice a Summer
Festival and not New York were you born in America

the inscrutable passage of a lawn-mower punctuates
the newly installed Muzack in the Shubert Theatre am I nuts
or is this the happiest moment of my life who's arguing it's
I mean 'tis lawd sakes it took daddy a long time to have
that accident so Ant Grace could get completely into black

didn't you know we was all going to be Zen Buddhists after
what we did you sure don't know much about war-guilt
or nothin and the peach trees continued to rejoice around
the prick which was for once authorized by our Congress
though inactive what if it had turned out to be a volcano

that's a mulatto of another nationality of marble
it's time for dessert I don't care what street this is
you're not telling me to take a tour are you
I don't want to look at any fingernails or any toes
I just want to go on being subtle and dead like life

I'm not naturally so detached but I think
they might send me up any minute so I try to be free
you know we've all sinned a lot against science
so we really ought to be available as an apple on a bough
pleasant thought fresh air free love cross-pollenization

oh oh god how I'd love to dream let alone sleep it's night
the soft air wraps me like a swarm it's raining and I have
a cold I am a real human being with real ascendancies
and a certain amount of rapture what do you do with a kid
like me if you don't eat me I'll have to eat myself

it's a strange curse my "generation" has we're all
like the flowers in the Agassiz Museum perpetually ardent
don't touch me because when I tremble it makes a noise
like a Chinese wind-bell it's that I'm seismographic is all
and when a Jesuit has stared you down for ever after you clink

I wonder if I've really scrutinized this experience like
you're supposed to have if you can type there's not much
soup left on my sleeve energy creativity guts ponderableness
lent is coming in imponderableness "I'd like to die smiling" ugh
and a very small tiptoe is crossing the threshold away

whither Lumumba whither oh whither Gauguin
I have often tried to say goodbye to strange fantoms I
read about in the newspapers and have always succeeded
though the ones at "home" are dependent on Dependable
Laboratory and Sales Company on Pulaski Street strange

I think it's goodbye to a lot of things like Christmas
and the Mediterranean and halos and meteorites and villages
full of damned children well it's goodbye then as in Strauss
or some other desperately theatrical venture it's goodbye
to lunch to love to evil things and to the ultimate good as "well"

the strange career of a personality begins at five and ends
forty minutes later in a fog the rest is just a lot of stranded
ships honking their horns full of joy-seeking cadets in bloomers
and beards it's okay with me but must they cheer while they honk
it seems that breath could easily fill a balloon and drift away

scaring the locusts in the straggling grey of living dumb
exertions then the useful noise would come of doom of data
turned to elegant decoration like a strangling prince once ordered
no there is no precedent of history no history nobody came before
nobody will ever come before and nobody ever was that man

you will not die not knowing this is true this year

1961

POEM

Lana Turner has collapsed!
I was trotting along and suddenly
it started raining and snowing
and you said it was hailing
but hailing hits you on the head
hard so it was really snowing and
raining and I was in such a hurry
to meet you but the traffic
was acting exactly like the sky
and suddenly I see a headline
LANA TURNER HAS COLLAPSED!
there is no snow in Hollywood
there is no rain in California
I have been to lots of parties
and acted perfectly disgraceful
but I never actually collapsed
oh Lana Turner we love you get up

1962

GALANTA

A strange den or music room
                    childhood
dream of Persian grass configured distilled
first hardon milky mess
                    the about-to-be
dead surrounding the already surrounded folk-
hero with a veil of automobile accidents
broken cocktail glasses
                    oh Sally
is still acting the mise en scene of her
great grandmother's embroidered graveyard
while I
                    my asiatic tendencies have taken me
to the Baghdad of neurasthenia and
false objectivity
                    faint hope for a familial
contrast for a far-reaching decadence
which presupposes unnatural unselfishness
your sweet yellow hair
                    among the mosques
the faint tribal twitch of your altered
blue eyes
                    when Canaan was reached you
called me France we threw sand in our eyes
and ran naked
                    down the street of our awful
progenitors
                    when life is fantastic there
is no chance for make-believe how lucky
the French bourgeois pain

                        could be if we
were children again and everything uninteresting
you never had a chance to be
                        Emma Bovary
nor I Julien Sorel in that attic in the States
and now
            I remember you only through American
Folk Art opening near the Fonda del Sol
where are you Sally with your practicality
and bottles of fireflies
                        blinking on
and off for footlights

                                        1962

FANTASY

(dedicated to the health of Allen Ginsberg)

How do you like the music of Adolph
                        Deutsch? I like
it, I like it better than Max Steiner's. Take his
score for *Northern Pursuit*, the Helmut Dantyne theme
was . . .
           and then the window fell on my hand. Errol
Flynn was skiing by. Down
                  down down went the grim
grey submarine under the "cold" ice.
                     Helmut was
safely ashore, on the ice.
              What dreams, what incredible
fantasies of snow farts will this all lead to?
                      I
don't know, I have stopped thinking like a sled dog.

The main thing is to tell a story.
                    It is almost
very important. Imagine
                throwing away the avalanche
so early in the movie. I am the only spy left
in Canada,
           but just because I'm alone in the snow
doesn't necessarily mean I'm a Nazi.
                  Let's see,
two aspirins a vitamin C tablet and some baking soda
should do the trick, that's practically an
                    Alka

Seltzer. Allen come out of the bathroom

                                  and take it.

I think someone put butter on my skis instead
of wax.

        Ouch. The leanto is falling over in the
firs, and there is another fatter spy here. They
didn't tell me they sent

                  him. Well, that takes care
of him, boy were those huskies hungry.

                          Allen,
are you feeling any better? Yes, I'm crazy about
Helmut Dantyne

            but I'm glad that Canada will remain
free. Just free, that's all, never argue with the movies.

                                1964

Artaud, Antonin. ANTHOLOGY
Bowles, Paul. A HUNDRED CAMELS IN THE COURTYARD
Burroughs, William & Ginsberg, Allen. THE YAGE LETTERS
CITY LIGHTS JOURNAL (No. 2)
CITY LIGHTS JOURNAL (No. 3)
Corso, Gregory. GASOLINE
Cossery, Albert. MEN GOD FORGOT
Dahlberg, Edward. BOTTOM DOGS
Daumal, René. MOUNT ANALOGUE
David-Neel, Alexandra. SECRET ORAL TEACHINGS IN TIBETAN BUDDHIST SECTS
Fenollosa, Ernest. THE CHINESE WRITTEN CHARACTER AS A MEDIUM FOR POETRY
Ferlinghetti. PICTURES OF THE GONE WORLD (PP. No. 1)
Ginsberg, Allen. HOWL AND OTHER POEMS (PP. No. 4)
Ginsberg, Allen. KADDISH AND OTHER POEMS (PP. No. 14)
Ginsberg, Allen. PLANET NEWS (PP. No. 23)
Ginsberg, Allen. REALITY SANDWICHES (PP. No. 18)
Hollo, Anselm. (Tr.) RED CATS (PP. No. 16)
Jasudowicz, Dennis. FLEA STREET AND OTHER PLAYS
Kaufman, Bob. DOES THE SECRET MIND WHISPER (Broadside)
Kaufman, Bob. GOLDEN SARDINE (PP. No. 21)
Kerouac, Jack. BOOK OF DREAMS
Lamantia, Philip. SELECTED POEMS (PP. No. 20)
Lowry, Malcolm. SELECTED POEMS (PP. No. 17)
Mailer, Norman. THE WHITE NEGRO
McClure, Michael. MEAT SCIENCE ESSAYS
Michaux, Henri. MISERABLE MIRACLE
O'Hara, Frank. LUNCH POEMS (PP. No. 19)
Olson, Charles. CALL ME ISHMAEL
Patchen, Kenneth. LOVE POEMS (PP. No. 13)
Patchen, Kenneth. POEMS OF HUMOR & PROTEST (PP. No. 3)
Pommy-Vega, Janine. POEMS TO FERNANDO (PP. No. 22)
Prévert, Jacques. PAROLES (PP. No. 9)
Rexroth, Kenneth. BEYOND THE MOUNTAINS
Rexroth, Kenneth (Tr.). THIRTY SPANISH POEMS OF LOVE & EXILE
Sanders, Ed. POEM FROM JAIL
Shure, Robert. TWINK
Solomon, Carl. MISHAPS, PERHAPS
Solomon, Carl. MORE MISHAPS
Svevo, Italo. JAMES JOYCE
Topor, Roland. PANIC (Drawings)
Watts, Alan W. BEAT ZEN, SQUARE ZEN, AND ZEN
Williams, William Carlos. KORA IN HELL: IMPROVISATIONS (PP. No. 7)